Erratic Fire, Erratic Passion

THE POETRY OF SPORTSTALK

Pasha Malla
& Jeff Parker

Introduction by Bethlehem Shoals

*f*eatherpr*oof* BOOKS

Published by
featherproof books
Chicago, Illinois
www.*featherproof*.com

First edition
10 9 8 7 6 5 4 3 2 1

Library of Congress Control Number: 2015946362
ISBN 13: 978-0983186342

Edited by Jason Sommer.
Design by Zach Dodson.
Proofread by Claire Gillespie.

Printed in Canada
Set in Perpetua

ROSTER

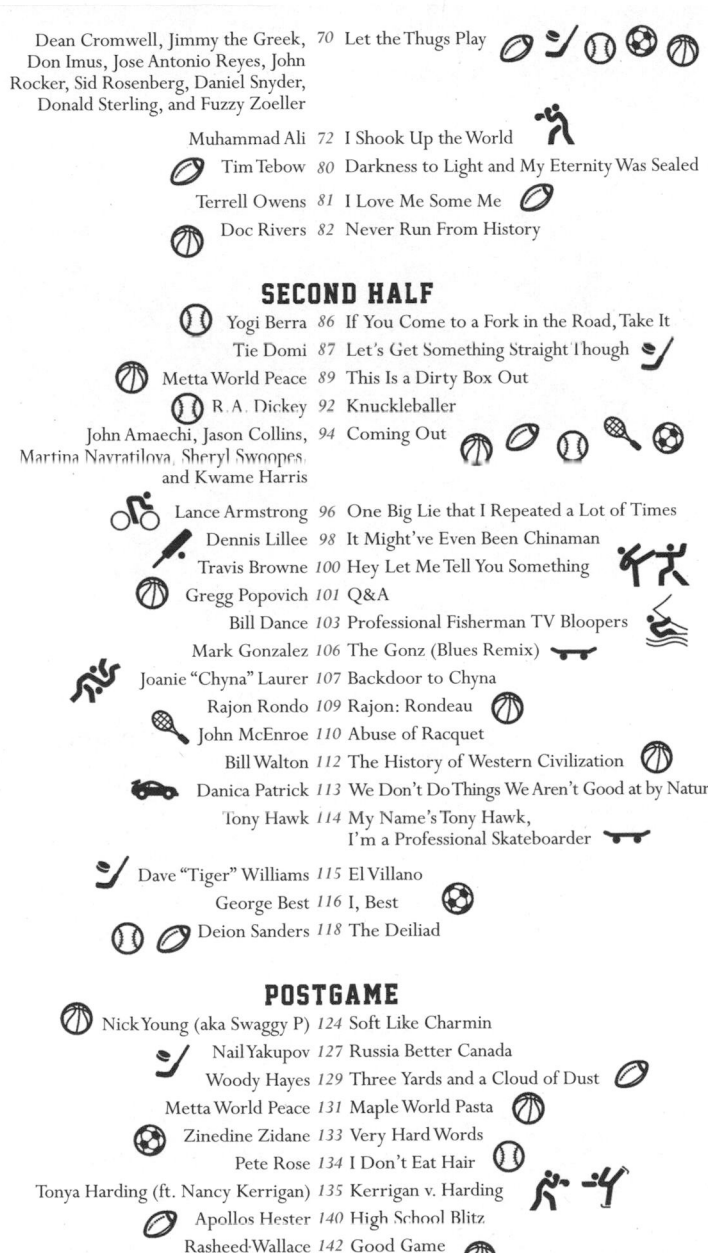

INTRODUCTION

More often than not, the language of sports is a formality. Saying is secondary to doing. We get a series of shared terms with minimal room for error or variation, whether in the rules that dictate how the game is played, or the way that the experience of playing or watching is described. Language is either the necessary condition for bodily heroism, or an unfortunate byproduct of it.

Nowhere is this more evident than in the athlete interview. Usually, athletes say what they think we want them to say, or what they've been told to say. Language is a skill, a deployment of banality that deflects or defangs questions from journalists. It is used to disguise both what the athlete really wants to say and what we, the audience, really want to hear. As a result, we get words that belong to no one in particular.

And yet every time an athlete tries to reveal as little as possible, he or she discloses *something*. Every evasion is self-reflexive. Every word represents a choice. As much as sports culture tries to deny it, language is more than a bunch of interchangeable parts that get you from Point A to Point B—or to the end of the interview.

Underneath it all, there's a ghost in the clichés, animating them, using them as a toolkit, and possibly even offering a glimpse into that elusive Real of sports. When an athlete blurts out a sentence, a word, or a phrase that tells us what they're really thinking, it reminds us that language in sports maintains a connection to some extremely powerful and unwieldy feelings. In these moments, we're forced to confront both the emotion of sports and our own resistance to it. We remember not just that athletes really care, in ways we can only begin to grasp, but that, all cynicism aside, we care that they care.

We are then forced to admit that there are human beings behind the veil of rote phrases. Sometimes it's a matter of excavation, sometimes decoding or close reading. In *Erratic Fire, Erratic Passion*, we see all of this at the same time. Reconfiguring the words of athletes converts scrambled or fragmentary language into plain-spoken truth. These poems aren't documents of collage or pastiche; nor are they translation or transcription. There's no required reading between the lines, grasping at insight, or hanging onto a single scrap of information. Instead, we get the athletes in their own words, articulated in a way that cuts through the bullshit and resolves the multiple layers of contradiction and distortion.

We can't ever really know what athletes are thinking. But we can use what they say to clarify who they are, to fill in the gaps of their personal stories and translate at least some of their action into words. We can't wring motivation out of platitudes but we can at least gain some perspective.

This book is a reconstruction. It provides a lens of understanding athletes by giving them the voice they may not have realized they had   or at least might have been reluctant to share with the world. The poems here turn the public record into an object for inquiry and an occasion for reflection. They offer proof that there are real people beneath the uniforms and beyond the prepackaged narratives. Athletes aren't like you or I, except in all the ways that they are. They are relatable and accessible insofar as they are human. And ultimately, that's what this book is about: Reminding us that in language, we can find common ground with individuals we're used to seeing as far-off, mythical figures. In *Erratic Fire, Erratic Passion*, the language of sports is reclaimed. You might even say that, for the first time, it's not a mere formality.

—***Bethlehem Shoals***

These poems were pieced together from the words of professional athletes. Quotations were taken mainly from online sources, primarily from countless hours of post-game/post-match interviews. Some of the poems have taken lines out of context and mixed them up while others are presented nearly verbatim. *Erratic Fire, Erratic Passion* is a mash-up/remix/ sampling project as much as anything, and we've taken the same liberties with the source material as a DJ might.

The athletes did not write the poems. Nothing here was authorized, prepared, approved, licensed, or endorsed by the athletes or by anyone on their behalf.

We hope that you enjoy reading what follows as much as we enjoyed "writing" it.

—*Pasha Malla & Jeff Parker*

PREGAME

ERRATIC FIRE, ERRATIC PASSION

Metta World Peace

I don't shake substitutions' hands.
I lose my feet.
I'd like to thank my psychiatrist.

I felt something,
But I didn't know it was an actual head.
I knew somebody suffered something at that point.
There were a lot of emotions in that game.
I can't worry about that.
I have to try to get the ball.

Kobe passed me the ball.
Kobe never passed me the ball.
And I could hear Phil Jackson—
He's the Zen master,
So you can just hear him in your head.
Saying, "Don't shoot don't shoot!"
And bam! I shot it.

I was lying down when I got hit with a liquid,
Ice and glass on my chest and on my face.
Nobody ever just threw anything at me
With the exception of a few times.

After that, it was self-defense.
I'll take the blame for that. It's my fault.
Stunned. So stunned. It's stunning.
Erratic fire, erratic passion.

We maximize it by playing together,
Loving each other,
Caring for each other.
Kind of like the Care Bears.
You know the Care Bears?
They care for each other.

I partied in July hard.
You got to party.
You can't just be a boring guy for twelve months, right?
You got to party hard in July.

Why are you staring at me, daughter?
Did you throw that?
Jack, you think we going to get in trouble?
Let me see
How I can answer your question
Without giving you a good quote.

SIXTY MINUTES OF PURE CHAOS

Ray Lewis

I got
a whole 'nother
fire
about myself.

I AM BEAUTIFUL, FAMOUS, AND GORGEOUS

Anna Kournikova

I am beautiful, famous, and gorgeous.
I have a lot of boyfriends,
I want you to write that.
Every country I visit,
I have a different boyfriend.
And I kiss them all.

A court is like a scene,
people want to see attractive people.
I think that tennis is a lady's sport,
so we should look out there like ladies.
It's true I always try
to be as seductive as possible,
but I wouldn't be here
if I couldn't play tennis.

I'm like a menu
at an expensive restaurant,
you can look at me,
but you can't afford me.

The world believes all blondes are stupid
and brunettes are smarter.
Well, I disagree.
Judgment is judgment,
whether you're obese,
or too skinny,
or not athletic enough.

I think it's really important for me
not to forget where I came from.
I grew up a little girl in the Soviet Union
playing at a small sports club.
At this year's Open,
I'll have five boyfriends.

YOU WOULD STILL LOOK AT ME AS A SCUMBAG

Mike Tyson

I don't know anything about that.
I don't know nothing about the numbers.
I just know what I can do.
Kill this motherfucker.

You can't touch me.
You're not man enough.
I eat your asshole alive, you bitch.
Fuck you, you ho.
Come and say it to my face.
And I fuck your ass in front of everybody.
You bitch.
Come on, you bitch.
You're scared, coward.
You're not man enough to fuck with me.
You can't last two minutes in my world, bitch.
Look at you,
Scared now, you ho.
Scared like a little white pussy.
Scared of the real man.
I'll fuck you till you love me, faggot.

I wish one of you guys had children
So I could kick them in the fucking head
Or stomp on their testicles
So you could feel my pain.
'Cause that's the pain I have,
Waking up every day.

I am a savage. I'm ferocious.
I just want to conquer people and their souls.
When I fight someone, I want to break his will.
I want to take his manhood.
I want to eat his children.
I'll take a bath in his blood.
If he's not dead, it doesn't count.
I want to rip out his heart and show it to him.

IF I WAS ELOQUENT WITH YOU

Mike Tyson

I hate Mike Tyson.
I don't like Mike Tyson.
I only wish the worst for Mike Tyson.

I'm a dreamer.
I have to dream and reach for the stars,
And if I miss a star then I grab a handful of clouds.

I don't think I have it anymore.
I don't got the fighting guts I don't think anymore.
I'm just sorry I let everybody down.
I just don't have this in my heart anymore.
I don't have that ferocity,
I'm not an animal anymore.
I'm not going to disrespect the sport anymore.

I don't love this no more. I don't love this no more.

I'm just tired of fighting.
If I have any anger,
If it's directed at anyone
It's directed at myself.
Because I'm disappointed in myself.

It left a great sting in my heart
And a great emptiness.

I want to be a better person in life.
I don't like the person who I've become.
I'm an insane individual.
I just want to be a decent human being,
Which I know I can be.

I'm sure I'll find something to do.
What I've done in the past is history.
And what I'm going to do in the future
Is a mystery.

PRACTICE

Allen Iverson

It's easy to sum it up when you just talk about Practice. We sitting here—I supposed to be the franchise player—and we in here talking about Practice. I mean, listen, we talking about Practice. Not a game, not a game. Not a game. We talking about Practice. Not a game. Not a, not a, not the game that I go out there and die for and play every game like it's my last. Not the game. We talking about Practice, man. I mean, how silly is that when we talking about Practice? I know I supposed to be there. I know I supposed to lead by example. I know that. And I'm not, I'm not shoving it aside, you know, like it don't mean anything. I know it's important. I do, I honestly do. But we talking about Practice, man. What are we talking about? Practice? We talking about Practice, man. We talking about Practice. We talking about Practice. We ain't talking about the game. We talking about Practice, man. When you come in the arena and you see me play, you see me play, don't you? You see me give everything I got, right? But we talking about Practice right now. We talking about Prac—. Man, look, I hear you. It's funny to me, too. It's strange, it's strange to me, too. But we talking about Practice, man. We not even talking about the game, the actual game. When it matters. We talking about Practice. How the hell can I make my teammates better by Practicing?

RICKEY HENDERSON FOR MAYOR OF OAKLAND

Rickey Henderson

I think the focus is on me
But I'm looking forward to the challenge
As far as the focus on me.

THE FIVE ELEMENTS

Rodger Schmidt, Wally Henry, Phill Drobnick, and John Benton

1.

It's important to understand
how we came up with the element concept.
And it really is a concept.

The best deliveries,
if you will,
have these elements in them.

Element one became setting up the stone
and setting up the body energy
based on the center of gravity.

The body generates most of the energy.

We looked at the body in relation to the stone.
That's important for energy and
that's important for balance.

The energy is lined at the target.
We tend to call that the energy line
because that's where you're focusing the energy.

You really want to make sure
that the stone and the body
are one in the sense of line.

At this point we're still talking about the body.

2.

In element two
the stone and the body
become one.

3.

Now the energy has been set.
The stone and the body are in motion.
How do you set up your body parts?
How do they fit together?

Obviously everyone has a different way
of doing almost everything.

Is it too far out?
Is it too far in?

It was not mechanical.
Mechanical teaching
led to mechanical behavior.

It is a game of feel.
Feel and touch and finish.
Putting your head together with your physical presence.

The thing I've found most fascinating about the
five elements is the energy.
You still have to maintain your energy
through the stone
the entire process.

Now you have elements one, two and three.

4.

Element four, quite simply:
Release.
Finish, we call it.

Eventually the stone has to go to the other end
instead of the body,
so the stone has to be released
on the generation line.

Okay, I understand the concept.
Now how does that fit me
as an individual?

Once I know my one or two details
in each element,
I know exactly what to work on—
and more importantly:
Why?

That isn't something I've put words to before.

5.

Element five,
a little harder to capture.

Element five:
How does the mind fit into all this?

You really have to tie your brain
into what you're doing.

Keep it: one, two, three, four, five.
And identify the simplest elements of that aspect.

We did a lot of review
and we kind of got a little more in depth
in each element.

The one element that I've seen
that we continue to work on
is the fifth element.

But the nice thing about the five elements
is you can put them into any delivery.

It really is a simplified way
of getting perfection.

FORD TOUGH

Don Cherry

I was made fun of 'cause I go to church,
I'm easy to do it that way.
One guy—a pink—called me a jerk,
So I thought I'd wear that for him today.

"Is that the kiss of death, that they give like that?"
I was asked, so I asked why.
I said, "I'm your man," right off the bat,
A famous, good-looking guy.

I was called maudlin because I honor the troops;
I guess that's what they do around here.
Put that in your pipe you left-wing kooks—
D'you expect Ron MacLean to come here?

In the morning they phoned me
And I was asked, "Why a landslide?"
I'm being ripped to shreds, but he's no phony,
all you pinkos out there that ride.

Rob's honest, he's truthful
He's like Julian Fantino.
The greatest Mayor Pit Bull
This city's ever seen-o.

FIRST HALF

MY WEAPON IS ME

Alexander Ovechkin

I'm only twenty and
I have a wagon and
A carriage full of power.
Russian machine never breaks.

I do anything.
I hit him.
I bite him.
My weapon isn't my shot.
It's me.

That's hockey.
You never know
What's going to happen.
It's a tough sport.
No tooth,
A broken nose,
But I'm looking good.

I wear tinted visor
Not to trick other players
But so hot girls in stands
Don't see me looking at them.

WHAT IS DEFENDING?

Johan Cruyff

If you have the ball,
you must make the pitch
as big
as possible.

If you lose the ball,
you must make the pitch
as small
as possible.

Everything is about meters.
That is all.

Make it…
playful.

Those who
can't be reached
don't participate.

Every disadvantage
has an advantage.
There's a lot
you can do now.

Defending is a matter of:
How much space
must I defend?

You can start crying.
So you better choose something else.

FROM THE PLANET LOVETRON...

Darryl Dawkins

The Funkadelic.
The Rim Wrecker.
The Spine Chiller Supreme.
The Look-Out-Below,
Cover-Your-Head,
In-Your-Face Disgrace.

The Mama Shakin'
Rim Breakin'
Teeth Shakin'
Get-Out-the-Wayin'
Backboard Swayin'
Game Delayin'
If-You-Ain't-Groovin'-
You-Best-Get-Movin'
Dunk.

The Yo Mama Special
The Go-Rilla
The Turbosexaphonic Delight
The Heartstopper
The Rump-roaster
The Bun-toaster
The Kickshaker
and
The Babymaker.

The Chocolate Thunder Flyin'
Glass Flyin'
Robinzine Cryin'
Parents Cryin'
Babies Cryin'
Cats Cryin'
Glass *Still* Flyin'
Thank-You-Ma'am,

Wham-Bam,
Glass-Breaker-I-Am
Jam.

Chocolate Thunder's
Takin' 'em under.

OPEN SECRETS

Venus and Serena Williams

Family is first
and nothing can come between that
because it's the basic unit of society.

> Family's first,
> and that's what matters most.
> We realize that our love goes
> deeper than the tennis game.

Tennis is just a game,
family is forever.

> There's no need for a feud
> to be going on,
> so I really don't have time for it.

If it was down to limbs,
they could take my limbs.
She has more going for her.
She has a great life.

> I know Serena's doing her best
> on the other side.

I always like to win.
But I'm the big sister.
I want to make sure she has everything,
even if I don't
have anything. It's hard.
I love her too much.
That's what counts.

> You know it's really hard.
> You have to get with someone
> who understands.

My first job is big sister
and I take that very seriously.

We never play
when no one's watching.
We always keep secrets.

Everyone makes
their own comments.
That's how rumors get started.

We were just like,
"Oh my god!"
Oh my goodness.

"Oh and Oh" is a tennis term.
It's a nice way of saying
you took your opponent to pieces.
If the sun comes up, I have a chance.

Rain is good for me.
I feel like I achieve clarity actually
when it rains.
The longer I have to sit and wait,
the clearer my game becomes to me.

You just do
the best you can do
and whatever
happens happens.

If you can keep playing tennis
when somebody is shooting a gun
down the street,
that's concentration.

At one point I was just thinking,
"I can't do this."

It wasn't fair at all.
I was just thinking,
"This is not fair."

I'm really exciting.
I smile a lot, I win a lot,
and I'm really sexy.
I've developed a karaoke habit.
No one likes getting their nails done
more than I do.

I have all the problems in the world.
I keep telling my therapist now,
"I want to be a physical therapist."

I always see stalkers on TV.
If I didn't play tennis
I don't know where I'd be.

I think I'm crazy
because I haven't slept that much.
I think I'm going to crash,
I just don't know when.
I could just fall out any second.

Nike makes the best shoes!

G.O.A.T.

Sudsy Monchik

When I was younger,
and for many years in the beginning,
I had major passion for the game.

Grew up in New York, as you know,
and the Parents owned a couple health clubs.
Just was always around the club.
I had a lot of success early.
It just kind of flowed into it.
It just kind of naturally happened.

I wanted to eat, sleep, drink—
all I did was think about racquetball.
Just wanted to play racquetball
as much as I could.

If I could sleep on the court,
I would—
I did—
I have.

And that lasted for many years.
And then that passion,
you know, burnt out,
like a candle.

People ask me if
I'm the greatest player
that ever played the game.
I finished No. 1 five times,
I played seven healthy seasons on tour.
Could I have done it ten times?
Could I have done it eight times?
You know, it's tough to say.

I would take me against
anybody in the world,
or out of this world for that matter.
One game—the best against the best.
But to answer the question,
Am I the best player ever?
I think so yeah.

THE ENFORCER

Georges Laraque

It does bother me.
You see my stats and
the zero looks bad.
A lot of the other tough guys
have at least scored a goal.

Animals don't stand in line
to get slaughtered,
to get killed.
But when I fight someone
on the ice,
I fight a millionaire.

Before I was vegan
I had high blood pressure
and had asthma,
and in just a couple of months
it was gone.

Any fight you get into you could die.
Milk clogs up your lungs.

CEMENT DOESN'T GIVE AS MUCH AS SNOW

Shaun White

It's pretty intense.
When you think about it,
We're strapping strange planks of wood to our feet
And launching off of giant snow walls.

When you think about it,
I wear black skinny-fit jeans
And launch off of giant snow walls.
I can't get away from them.

I wear black skinny-fit jeans.
I trip walking down the stairs.
I can't get away from them.
But I can skate them probably.

I trip walking down the stairs.
It's pretty intense.
But I can skate them probably.
We're strapping strange planks of wood to our feet.

101-DECIBEL GRUNT HAIKU

Maria Sharapova

Uhhhhh! Angh! Angh! Uhhhhh! Ahhhh!
Awahhhhh! Eeeeeee! Awahhhhh! Unhhhhhhhhhhhhhh! Eeeeeee!
Aaaaaiiiiiieeeee! Angh! Angh! Unhhhhhhhh!

THE GONZ

Mark Gonzalez

It's kind of nice to think about art and skateboarding
As a way of conquering boredom. Kind of like the blues.
People being bummed out or not having anything to do...
So what do they do? Ride a skateboard or they make art or
They write a letter to God even though God won't read the letter.
So there's not much you can do in life except do art and skate.

I have a hard time trying to communicate with people.
That's why I think that, a lot of times, skateboarding was a way
For me to communicate with something that was not alive
But it was still my friend, like a skateboard.

I like moving a lot.
My thing is,
I like to always move.
When you stay still, get stagnant,
People can see you in that spot
And peg you.
But if you're always moving
It's hard for them to get you.
That's right that's right
bad boy coming through.
That's right
bad boy coming through.

Learn new tricks.
Learn harder tricks.
Do 'em faster
Do 'em more powerful
Do 'em more finesseful
Do 'em—
Don't get hurt.

The whole idea
Is to break the laws of gravity

And to move in a way that—
to show that you can move
in a way that's not normal.

WELL I'M FEELING VERY HAPPY TODAY

Jahangir Khan

Well actually I born with hernia
and when I was very young I was so weak
when I had actually two operation as well.

My doctor say to my father, you know,
"He can't play any tough game."

So anyway because I was just playing,
just, you know,
I didn't tell my father
but I was just playing
slowly slowly game.

But I was so interesting,
you know,
because my family game.
And that was actually
my hobby, you know?

Well actually
I had a really bad start
because I actually
injured my back.

Well it was really
big shock for me.
I have to take rest for
one week, two weeks.

Then I was keep winning.
I was keep getting more confident.

Really I was really
thank to the Allah.

I just wanted to play.

MULTIPLE HERSCHELS

Herschel Walker

I dissociated when I was a kid.
Being bullied, being overweight,
Being picked on,

Not loving myself.
If a pencil fell on the floor
I would jump.

People think I was trying to commit suicide.
That was the farthest thing from my mind.
I was rolling. I was in tall cotton.

I created all these alters within myself.
I created a whole team within myself.
I probably have a bunch of them today.

I've incorporated this guy into me.
It's not the Herschel with pieces,
This is Herschel as a whole now.

I wrote everything.
I write down everything.
I created a toy.

BATS AND TREES

Brad Keselowski

I think of racing—
and this is a little bit
of like Confucius
so just bear with me.
I think of racing as though
you're running through the woods.
And if you stop
there's this guy chasing you
that hits you with a baseball bat.
Every time you stop
he hits you with it.
But the important thing
to remember along the way
is to not confuse
running into a tree
with being hit by the bat.
They're both made out of wood
and they both hurt.
One's your fault
one's not.
And I would say
going back to that instant,
I didn't hit him with a bat
he ran into a tree.
I make a lot of trees.
I plant trees around my competitors.
How about that?

THE GREAT WHITE HOPE

Larry Bird

As far as playing,
I didn't care who guarded me—
Red, yellow, black.
I just didn't want a white guy guarding me,
Because it's disrespect to my game.

I really got irritated when they put a white guy on me.
I still don't understand why.
A white guy would come out,
I would always ask him,
"What, do you have a problem with your coach?
Did your coach do this to you?"
And he would say, "No," and I'd say,
"Come on,
You got a white guy coming out here to guard me;
You got no chance."

And for some reason
That always bothered me
When I was playing against a white guy.

SLAUGHTERHOUSE IN A BLOUSE

Ronda Rousey

I don't really care. I don't still wear blouses. Getting rapped about by Eminem is like getting arm-barred by me. It might not be pleasant if you're on the other side of it, but it's so skillfully done you have to be honored. It's not like this is rocket science. This is fighting. I love fighting. I'm a fighter. There's something innately human about fighting. People have been fighting each other for millennia. It's part of human nature. It's preserving something that's real, that I think is trying to be crushed out of society. And I think it's the safest way that we can keep it. People need to hold on to their sanity somehow. The gym is my safe place. It's where I retain my sanity. It was the guys in the gym who made me be more fashionable. It's funny that it was the men who really girlied me up instead of the other way around. I was broke, I couldn't buy anything, but as soon as I made a little bit of money they took me under their Armenian wings. I've been broke as fuck, but I've never owed anyone shit. It's hard to sit back and be proud yet. I'm scared all the time. You have to have fear in order to have courage. I'm a courageous person because I'm a scared person. I was never very popular in school. I would go to school and be like this introverted loser kid that no one really knew. I was unhappy and thought that when I got the right body I would be happy. But I was going at it backwards. I had to make myself happy first and then the body came. Happiness is the absence of wants. I might not be perfect, but parts of me are pretty awesome. So if I was an X-Men I'd probably be Wolverine. I speak really, really fast because the people in my family all had very interesting things to say, and so I learned to say what I want to say loud and really fast because that's the only way I was going to break in and be heard. What other words can I use that won't change the meaning? What I'm going to do is convince you that it's a good idea to move in the direction I want you to go. Can I swear on this? I mean, come on. You trying to play that game with me? Tell me anything clever you can think of. I got three sisters, man, and a mom with a PhD. There's no way any of these girls who get punched in the face for a living can out-argue me. I don't feel bad at all. I defended myself very well. She's a cute chick. She chose to have her arm broken. I was technically in a kidnap situation. I just said I could beat up both her and her boyfriend in the same day. So they sued me. Whatever. The confusing thing is we now live in a society where it's not illegal to be an asshole, but it's illegal to slap one. People live such soft lives now. When was the last time something rough even touched your skin? Sometimes we need to get a little bit hurt just to be reminded that we're still human. I don't enjoy hurting people but it's part of my job. I was fighting in flip-flops, like you do. Everyone was losing shoes. Somebody got hurt. It was one of those things that most girls go through. I was feeding a falcon. Never sneeze in front of a falcon. Is that such an unbelievable thing to say?

CARL LEWIS

Ben Johnson

This guy's attitude
Is like fantasy stuff.
His foot went from a size 9
To a size 12 in one year.
If he can't come face to face
We know what he is.
Carl Lewis is just an envious
And a jealous man.
He is not a man.
He cannot give credit
To any sprinter
Who is better than he is.
That's just how he is.
He has to live with that conscience
And that conscience is a lie
And he knows that.
I am not afraid of Carl.
He's always inventing some excuse.
He can't admit someone's beating him.
He is not going to come forward
Because he is not a man.

BEN JOHNSON

Carl Lewis

You look at the old westerns,
They have the guy in the white hat
And the guy in the black hat.
I felt that being the clean guy
I was the guy in the white hat.
I was trying to beat this evil guy.
You know the guy's doing drugs,
He's big as a house.
You've got to be kidding me.
This is ridiculous.
I was so whatever.
I was just like, "Whatever."
Get over it, charge it to the game.
Like I said, get over it. If you can't
Charge it to the game,
You got played.
Then build a bridge.
At the end of the day
Someone who cheats
Has a lower moral standard
Than someone who does not.
And they will cheat
In other areas of life as well.

WORLD'S YOUNGEST MONSTER TRUCK DRIVER, AGE 7

Kid KJ

Monster Bear.
'Cause it's a monster truck.
Because I'm a kid.
2,500 pounds.
Seven feet high.
Get on the floor-length bar
And then get on the tire
And then get in.
It hydraulic lifts up.
A full roll cage.
And all the controls.
They have a special sixth
Brakes so it can stop me
Faster than regular car brakes.
A full roll cage and
A five-point safety
Harness seat belt and
A HANS device and a helmet.
I have a fire suit.
Jumping cars.
Donuts.

IT IS WHAT IT IS

Charles Oakley

I'm a grown man.
I do grown things.

I speak the truth, I'm about the truth
And I'm not a bullshitter.

If you don't know facts
You shouldn't even interview me

Because I'm gonna expose you
Because it's bullshit.

If you have a horse that isn't winning any races
Sooner or later you have to get a new jockey.

We're not going to go there and lay an egg
Because we already had the chicken.

I'll just keep eating my bread, sipping my soup
And serving my time.

But the chicken is going to lay
Some more eggs one day. Mayonnaise is overrated.

It's like having a car with new tires:
Say one tire wear, you buy four—

No. You wait till all them wear, then buy 'em.
Old ain't nothing.

You've got new cars that break down
And old cars that pass them.

You want to rob the bank
But you better not be complaining when you get caught.

I'm like the cops. I'm here to serve.
When you need some, I'll come to your rescue.

Like the police trying to stop a shootout:
You gotta have your gun out.

Don't go out there
With your hands down.

Drink your milk
And go to sleep.

HALFTIME

HOW BEAT UP ARE YOU?

Kevin Garnett

I'm beat up,
John. I'm beat up.
I'm beat up.
I'm—
I'm beat up.

I'm out there,
I suit up every night.
I suit up every night.
Banged up, hurt, whatever.

A hundred percent, thirty percent:
Ain't no numbers.
It's in my heart
And you can't measure that.

I'm losing.
I'm losing.
I'm losing.
I'm losing.

I WASN'T GOING VERY FAST, BUT UNFORTUNATELY I HIT A FEW THINGS

Tiger Woods

I'm the one who did those things:
Chase a little white ball around and work on my farmer's tan.
But you strip away the denial, the rationalization,
You become disgusting.
I tried to stop and I couldn't stop.
If you keep doing that each and every year
You're going to have one heck of a career.
I absolutely killed it, but I didn't know if it carried or not.
All you do is stay alive.
I'm trying to win every tournament I play.
I've always wanted to dye my hair blond.
As far as a burden on my life,
I'm trying to become a better person, each and every day.
I don't have any more shots to play. I'm done.

HINDSIGHT IS A WONDERFUL THING

David Beckham

I have got this obsessive compulsive disorder

Where I have to have everything in a straight line or
Everything has to be in pairs.

We've been asked to do *Playboy* together,
Me and Victoria, as a pair.

I don't think I'll ever go naked,
But I'll never say never.

I always wanted to be a hairdresser.
I like nice clothes, whether they're dodgy or not.

My parents have been there for me ever since I was about 7.

Soccer is a magical game.
Nothing amazes me anymore.

CALL ME MUNI

Munenori Kawasaki

I grew up in Japan!
I am Japanese!

What is up?
This is too much fun!

*I absolutely can't believe
the way that I've been accepted
by the players here,
by the fans.*

Thank you.

My English isn't good enough
but I am every day
studying English.

*For this one strange Japanese guy,
to come here and be accepted, the way I have,
has really been an unbelievable experience.*

Because…
I don't know.
English, no.

I am study, yeah.

Thank you very much!

Better better every day.
Practice.

Yeah, thank you very much!

I'm not dying or anything.

It's just that tomorrow
the field will be different.

See you tomorrow.
Don't touch my mustache.

LET THE THUGS PLAY

Dean Cromwell, Jimmy the Greek, Don Imus, Jose Antonio Reyes, John Rocker,
Sid Rosenberg, Daniel Snyder, Donald Sterling, and Fuzzy Zoeller

How about your whole life, everyday,
you could do whatever you want.
You can sleep with them,
you can do whatever you want.
The little I ask is not to promote it
and not to bring them to
my games.

I'm not a racist or prejudiced person
But certain people bother me.

The black is a better athlete to begin with
because he's been bred to be that way.
The slave owner would breed
his big black
to his big woman
so that he could have a big black kid.

It was not long ago
that his ability to sprint and jump
was a life-and-death matter to him
in the jungle. His muscles are pliable,
and his easy-going disposition is a valuable aid
to the mental and physical relaxation
that a runner and jumper must have.

You pat him on the back
and say congratulations
and enjoy it and tell him
not to serve fried chicken next year.

The girls from Rutgers, they got tattoos.
That's some nappy-headed hos,
I'll tell you that now.

The girls from Tennessee, they all look cute,
kind of like a Spike Lee thing:
The Jigaboos Versus the Wannabes—
that movie that he had.

There's nothing wrong with minorities,
they're fabulous.
My theory is that the black crowd
scared away the whites.
The kiss cam is too black.

Demuestra que eres mejor
que ese negro de mierda.

I SHOOK UP THE WORLD

Muhammad Ali

1.

The man to beat me
hasn't been born yet.
I'm not the greatest;
I'm the double greatest.
Not only do I knock 'em out,
I pick the round.

Well Henry Cooper is nothing
but a tramp.
He's a bum.
I'm the world's greatest.
He must fall in five rounds
but if he talk about me
I'll cut it to three.
After I'm through beating him,
I think he'll have to
join the Beatles and
be a singer.

Joe Frazier's in trouble.
'Cause the Muhammad Ali
Joe Frazier is going to meet
is going to be better
than the Muhammad Ali
he met three years ago.

Joe's going to come out smokin'
and I ain't gonna be jokin'
I'll be peckin' and a pokin'
pouring water on his smokin'.
Now this might shock and amaze ya
but I will destroy Joe Frazier.
Some people say, "You better watch Joe Frazier,

he's awful strong."
I say, "Tell him to try Ban Roll-On."
(That's deodorant.)

I'm going to do something to Joe Frazier that might be illegal.
My lawyers told me
to bring a bail bondsman to get me out of jail.
They might put my tail in jail
and get me out on bail
after what I do to Joe Frazier.

Frazier is so ugly
he should donate his face
to the US Bureau of Wildlife.
Frazier is so ugly that
when he cries,
the tears turn around and
go down the back of his head.
It will be a killer,
and a chiller,
and a thriller,
when I get the gorilla
in Manila.
I always bring out the best
in men I fight,
but Joe Frazier,
I'll tell the world right now,
brings out the best in me.

I've seen George Foreman
shadow boxing
and the shadow won.
Floats like a butterfly,
sting like a bee,
his hands can't hit
what his eyes can't see.
Now you see me,
now you don't.
George thinks he will,

but I know he won't!
It's a divine fight.
This Foreman—
he represents Christianity,
America,
the flag.
I can't let him win.
He represents pork chops.
That all you got, George?

Sonny Liston is nothing.
The man can't talk.
The man can't fight.
The man needs
talking lessons.
The man needs
boxing lessons.
And since he's gonna fight me,
he needs falling lessons.
Get up sucker and fight.
Get up and fight.

I predict that this will be Buster's last stand.
I will do to Buster
What the Indians did to Custer.
Wipe him out.

I done wrestled with an alligator,
I done tussled with a whale,
only last week I murdered a rock,
injured a stone,
hospitalized a brick.
I'm so mean I make medicine sick.
I'm so fast that last night
I turned off the light switch
in my hotel room and
was in bed before the room
was dark.
I am the astronaut of boxing.

Joe Louis and Dempsey
were just jet pilots.
I'm in a world of my own.
There are two things that
are hard to hit and see.
That's a spooky ghost
and Muhammad Ali.

2.

Why should they ask me
to put on a uniform
and go 10,000 miles from home
and drop bombs
and bullets
on brown people
while so-called Negro people
in Louisville
are treated like dogs?
I got nothing against
no Viet Cong.
No Vietnamese
ever called me a nigger.
Boxing is a lot of white men
watching two black men
beat each other up.

Cassius Clay is a slave name.
I didn't choose it
and I don't want it.
I am Muhammad Ali,
a free name—
it means beloved of God—
and I insist
people use it
when people speak
to me and
of me.

What's my name, fool?
What's my name?

Boxing was only for self-gain,
just beating up one of my brothers
or somebody else's brother
for money.
Possibly hurting 'em for life,
which I didn't intend to do and
I'm lucky I never really did.
I would say I get more pleasure
converting so-called negroes.
I enjoy this much better than boxing.

I always asked my mother,
I said, "Momma, how come
is everything white?"
I said, "Why is Jesus white
with blond hair and blue eyes?
Why is the Lord's Supper all white men?
Angels are white.
Mary and even the angels."
I said, "Mother, when we die
do we go to heaven?"
She said, "Naturally we go to heaven."
I said, "Well what happened to all the black angels?
They took the pictures?"
I said, "Oh, I know, if the white folks
were in heaven, too,
then the black angels were in the kitchen
preparing the milk and honey."
She said, "Listen, you quit saying that, boy."
I was always curious
and I always wondered
why I had to die to go to heaven.
Couldn't have pretty cars and
good money and nice homes *now*.
Why do I have to wait
'til I die to get milk and honey?

And I said, "Momma, I don't want
no milk and honey.
I like steaks and..."
I said, "Milk and honey's
a laxative anyway.
Do they have a lot of bathrooms in heaven?"
So anyway I was always curious.
I always wondered why, you know,
Tarzan is the King of the Jungle in Africa—
he was white.
I saw this white man swinging
around Africa with a diaper on hollering,
"aah-eeh-ah-eeh-aaaaaah!"
And here's Tarzan talking to the animals
and the African's been there for centuries
and he can't talk to the animals.
I always wondered why Miss America
was always white.
All the beautiful brown women in America
beautiful suntans
beautiful shapes all types of complexions
but she always was white
and Miss World was always white
and Miss Universe was always white.
and then they got some stuff called
White House Cigars
White Swan Soap
King White Soap
White Cloud Tissue Paper
White Rain Hair Rinse
White Tornado Floor Wax.
Everything was white.
And the Angel Food Cake was the white cake.
And the Devil Food Cake was the chocolate cake.
I said, "Momma, why is everything white?"
I always wondered.
And the president lived in the White House
and Mary had a little lamb
whose fleece was white as snow

and Snow White
and everything was white.
And Santa Claus was white.
And everything bad was black.
The little ugly duckling was a black duck
and the black cat was the bad luck
and if I threaten you
I'm gonna blackmail you.
I said, "Momma why don't
they call it whitemail?
They lie, too."
I was always curious
and then—this is when
I knew something was wrong.
Won the Olympic gold medal in Rome, Italy.
Olympic champion—the Russian's
standing right here
and the Pole right here.
I'm defeating America's
so-called threats
or enemies.
And the flag is going
dun dun dun dun dun dun
dun dun dun dun dun
I'm standing so proud
dun-dun duuun dun dun dun
and I done whooped the world for America
Dun dun dun dun dun
I took my gold medal,
thought I'd invented something.
I said, "Man, I know I'm going to
get my people freed today.
I'm the Champion of the whole world.
Olympic champion.
I know I can eat downtown now
and I went downtown that day,
had my big ole medal on,
went into a restaurant.
At that time things weren't integrated.

Black folks couldn't eat downtown
and I went downtown.
I sat down
and I said, "A cup of coffee, a hotdog…"
The lady said, "We don't serve negroes."
I was so mad,
I said, "I don't eat them either
just give me a cup of coffee and a hamburger"
I said, "I'm the Olympic gold medal—
won three days ago. I fought for this country in Rome
and I'm gonna eat."
I had to leave that restaurant
in my hometown
where I went to church
and served in their Christianity
and fought—and daddy fought in all the wars—
just won the gold medal
and couldn't eat downtown.
I said, "Something's wrong."

3.

You want me to get some gloves on, boy?
I'm the prettiest fighter in the ring today.
That's my label.
There's not a man alive
who can whup me.
I'm too fast.
I'm too smart.
I'm too pretty.
I should be a postage stamp.
That's the only way I'll ever get licked.
It's hard to be humble,
When you're as great as I am.
I'm ready to back up
everything I'm saying
And I'm through talking.

DARKNESS TO LIGHT AND MY ETERNITY WAS SEALED

Tim Tebow

Growing up actually
my parents didn't let us
have desserts a lot.

But every Sunday
when we got home from church
we were able to eat as much
ice cream as we wanted.

So we'd go on the couch and watch football
and eat ice cream together
and we'd eat a lot.

And I still love eating ice cream
although I try not to have it as much now.

But I still love it.

I LOVE ME SOME ME

Terrell Owens

I don't want that to be the headline.
I'm human;
That's what people don't realize.
I don't have no friends.
I don't want no friends.
I don't have to play football.
I don't see outside of me.

NEVER RUN FROM HISTORY

Doc Rivers

I told our guys,
"Tonight we're fighting human nature."
I told them,
"I'm telling you,
we're fighting human nature tonight.
That team is coming after you
with everything they have,
and I don't know if you can match that."
And at the end of the day,
we did not.

SECOND HALF

IF YOU COME TO A FORK IN THE ROAD, TAKE IT

Yogi Berra

If you don't know where you're going,
you'll end up somewhere else.

LET'S GET SOMETHING STRAIGHT THOUGH

Tie Domi

I've been misquoted
about a few things
that kind of really ticked me off.

It'd be like that interview.
Who's that one guy that
interviewed that one guy
on that talk show?
They went right at it on TV.

Like holy cripe,
you know?
Are they paying you or something?

I've never said
anything bad about Winnipeg, at all.
I never said once in a million years,
"Winnipeg,"
ever.

You know,
my whole career has been like that.
You know I've been misquoted
and whatnot. But that's just professional sports.
You learn to accept it.

It makes you mentally tougher.
It does.
I don't even read
the newspapers now.
If it's there
I'll look at it
and read it.
You know I don't really read
those stories.

That's good.
I like that.

THIS IS A DIRTY BOX OUT

Metta World Peace

1.
Spitting up blood
And coughing up blood,
I'm not going to call it in.
Growing up as a kid,
I remember playing
In Far Rockaway.
There's only
One way in,
One way out.

Far Rockaway is like the
New Orleans of New York.
I never back down
So I play hard.
My man got hit over the head
With a bottle
—BOOM—
At the free-throw line
While he's shooting
Free throws.
Bats and guns come out.
We got to get out.

It's not like I brung this
Aggression to the league.
I didn't invent this.
We grew up wanting
To play with passion.
So when the guys say,
We're dirty,
We're just playing hard.
We're not playing dirty.
We're just playing.

What am I
Supposed to do?
Skinny up?
The guys can take
Every little clip and,
"This is a dirty box out,
This is a dirty box out."
That impact is not soft.
It hurts me, too.

2.

I've got to get
Some of this TV time.
All these cameras.
Follow me on Twitter.
I need a million followers.
Kobe should tweet for game two
The whole time,
Every possession.
Critique us,
Criticize us,
Chew us out.
I'll tweet him back.
I'll direct message him.
Kobe's a great tweeter.
I don't follow him.
I don't follow Kobe
Because all I follow
Is four people.
I follow the Dalai Lama
And I follow a couple
Other people.

3.

Whether it's a free country or not,
You should be free to act

As you want to do
As long as it's not violent.
No matter what it is.
I came here in
A Cookie Monster shirt
Because I wanted to,
And I was going
To wear the pants.
But I thought you guys
Were going to judge me.
I was going
To wear the hat, too.
But I thought you guys
Would judge me.
So that's why I didn't
Wear the hats and the pants.
But I should've wore it.
You should be free
To do and act
How you want to act.

KNUCKLEBALLER

R.A. Dickey

They know what they're getting.
I know what I'm throwing.
It's just a matter of
Can I throw a good one?

A knuckleball is antithetical
To any other conventional pitch
In the sense that
Conventional pitching is meant to
Impart spin unto the baseball.

A knuckleball is different than that
In the sense that you're trying to
Subtract spin completely.

A perfect knuckleball for me
Will rotate about a quarter of a revolution
From the time it leaves my hand
To the time it gets to the plate.

Oh mercy.
I wish I would've kept track
Of how many pitches I threw
Against a cinder-block wall somewhere
Trying to learn the mechanics
The grip
The way it feels as it leaves your hand
The pressure you need to put on
Your forefinger and
Your fingernails
I mean, it took
So many repetitions.
And I stunk
For a while.

I always held onto the hope.
It was dark.
It was a dark period for a little while for me
Because I was an older guy
Trying to learn this new thing
And not making much money
And trying to figure it all out.

We call this the horseshoe of the baseball
For obvious reasons.
I take my fingernail
Of my pointer finger and middle finger
And I dig it into the leather
Right behind the seam.
And I keep my thumb off the seam
On the side
So it doesn't want to spin.
I keep my wrist locked at
As close to a ninety-degree angle
As I can.

And then
When I throw it
I just kind of bring
My hand forward
Just a little bit.
And I release it at
The opportune moment.
But that opportune moment
Has taken a long time to
Figure out when that is.

COMING OUT

John Amaechi, Jason Collins, Kwame Harris, Martina Navratilova,
and Sheryl Swoopes

You know that
the sky's blue
but you keep
telling yourself
that it's red.

As you keep
playing you
realize that you
have to maintain
this sort of mask,

that you have
to continue to
compartmentalize
different aspects
of yourself

in a way your
straight teammates
don't have to.
When you do
something bad

you're a wuss
or a fag
or a wuss.
You don't want
to be that distraction.

The kind of contact
that goes on in locker rooms,
The kind of intimacy
that goes on between men—
it's as gay as it gets.

I would look around the locker room
and think, "And *I'm* the gay one?"
It takes so much energy to be hiding who you are.
And girls who are good at sports, it's almost treated
that if you're good at sports you can't be a girl.

Sport has been gay since Homer.
There's not much difference
between a gay athlete and a straight athlete
aside from what they desire,
what they seek pleasure in.

When you finally get to that point of acceptance
there's nothing more beautiful.
It was such a great sense of relief:
This is who I am. It's a great feeling.
For the first time I had this notion of liberation awaiting me.

I've been trying to figure out what it means to be gay.
It's an everyday word now. It doesn't matter that you're gay.
Now you're getting support when you come out.
We don't have to hide, it's incredible.
You just try to live an honest, genuine life.

There's some kid who's not going to commit suicide.
They will play better ball. He's going to save lives.
It's all about dedication.
I don't really care about everybody else.
I'm ready to raise my hand.

ONE BIG LIE THAT I REPEATED A LOT OF TIMES

Lance Armstrong

I have been on my deathbed,
and I'm not stupid.
I can emphatically say,
I am not on drugs.

I do not take performance-enhancing drugs.
Why would I enter into a sport
and then dope myself up
and risk my life again?
That's crazy.
I would never do that.
No way.

I have never doped.
I can say it again,
but I've said it for seven years.
How many times do I have to say it?
Well, it can't be any clearer than
"I've never taken drugs."

As long as I live, I will deny it.
There was absolutely no way
I forced people,
encouraged people,
told people,
helped people,
facilitated. Absolutely not.
One hundred percent.

We are completely innocent.
The simple truth
is that we outwork everyone.

If you're trying to hide something,
you wouldn't keep getting away

with it for ten years.
Never failed a test.
I rest my case.

IT MIGHT'VE EVEN BEEN CHINAMAN

Dennis Lillee

I'm not a statistical person.
Some of those can tell a lie.

It was one that we'd planned
going wider on the crease
and angling right across
where the slip's a little wider—
and it worked.
It gave me a lot of pleasure.

More than anything else
I was probably a little embarrassed.
I wasn't thinking
so I ended up going
to no man's land.

I didn't feel that well.
Maybe it was the twelve Weetabix I had for breakfast,
I'm not sure.
But I really didn't feel that well.

I had three guys out there.
It was almost like they were
willing you on.

It was a great feeling
but you probably think,
"Well it's happened to other people,"
and all that other sort of stuff.

But upon reflection it probably
was one of the first of its kind.

Why they took me to their heart I don't know.
Maybe it was the rebellious streak.
I mean, I always made myself available.

Maybe all those things
would help them
take you to their heart.

HEY LET ME TELL YOU SOMETHING

Travis Browne

The only difference about
Us in here and you guys out
There is we're about
Braver for about
Fifteen minutes longer.

Q&A

Gregg Popovich

Q:

A: Happy? Happy? Am I being punked or something? I don't know how to judge happy. We're in the middle of a contest. Nobody's happy. This is all business. I want some nasty. To say anything less than that would be disingenuous. Getting to the point where you slap yourself—and you don't cry about it or pity yourself—and move on.

Q:

A: No second question, huh? I'm hurt. I need a little bit more of a dose of nasty. Gimme, gimme. Gimme? Gimme? My kids used to say, "Gimme." I would correct them all the time.

Q:

A: That's a third question, isn't it? Don't you just get two? I hesitate to tell you why I think we'll win or won't win. I have no clue what is going to happen tonight. All I can do is hope. I have no idea what the outcome of the game will be. We're older than dirt, number one. I'm old. My hand shakes. Your hand shouldn't shake. Relax. I have more time. In the heat of the game stuff comes out of my mouth and sometimes it's embarrassing. That's why I always say coaches are sick puppies.

Q:

A: "How big is it?" How do I measure that? Is it like one through ten? You going to ask me about calculus next? Science would infer some sort of logical and consistent and intellectual concern, but I don't think that's true. I really don't think that's true. Science is probably too strong a word. We're not that smart. It's not supposed to be easy. Are we having fun yet?

Q:

A: It's a big boy game. It's torture. It's hard to appreciate or enjoy torture. So why do we do it? We're sick puppies.

Q:

A: That's the best question any of these people have ever asked me. That's the best news I've heard all day. This is one of the joys of my life right here. This is great fun. There's nothing I would rather be doing. And the questions are so incisive and well thought out, how could one not enjoy trying to find the answer? I was waiting for the question. I thought I was pretty patient: "I'll take some time, I'll walk the streets some place. I'll spend some time with my family in other places." You can only grow so many tomatoes and read so many books. But it finally came. The question finally came. I think that's a great question. What was the question?

Q:

A: Geez oh whiz guys, come on. Think of a question. You have any questions, young man? Come on, think of one. Anything. Show me some nasty.

Q:

A: I'll just pass on that one. I'm going to get a bite to eat and have a ... a Gatorade. That's what I'm supposed to drink, right? Have a good night.

PROFESSIONAL FISHERMAN TV BLOOPERS

Bill Dance

There's many different types of bait
that can be used for situations like this.
Dagummit.

You know
before you ever wet a line
you should always
and I mean always
put some thought about
what you gonna do.
Shoot.

Watch that stump.
Watch that stump.
Dagummit.
I didn't mean reverse it that strong.
I said, watch the stump.

Repeated casts
to the same place.
The fish are inactive
first of all.
Dagummit.

Golly.
Come here.
Ah.
Come here, you.
Whoo.
Man.

A rod that's lightweight
that's extremely sensitive.
Dagummit.
Oh it's sensitive all right.

It's sensitive enough
I felt that fan.
Dagummit.
Get another rod.

Just little short jigs
or other times
sweeping it
let it work.
Doggone it.
Oh man.

Pull up. Pull up.
Pull up. Pull up.
Pull up, Kenny!

So if you've got
fifteen feet of water
you want to let your—
It's real funny.
Take your shotgun mic
And stick it where
the sun don't shine.

Blue Lizard gives you
maximum protection.
What the hell was that?

Get under a shade tree.
Eat a little snack.
I'll tell you one thing:
It really can help you.

We've got our tackle box.
We've got our cooler.
And we've got our battery.
Dagummit.

Oh gosh.

Ow that hurts.
Oh, it's past the barb.
Call the doctor.

THE GONZ (BLUES REMIX)

Mark Gonzalez

It's kind of nice to think about art and skateboarding
As kind of like the blues.
People being bummed out or not having anything…
Bad boy coming through.

So they write a letter to God but stay still, get stagnant.
I like to always move.
Skateboarding was a way for me to communicate:
Bad boy coming through.

The whole idea is God won't read the letter.
So in life, what do they do?
Learn new tricks. Learn harder tricks.
Bad boy coming through.

That's right, that's right:
Bad boy coming through.

BACKDOOR TO CHYNA

Joanie "Chyna" Laurer

It was just never my thing:
I had never even watched a porn.
I have a lot of fans.
I never thought I was as beautiful
as they were. For me it's kind of a little fairy tale life.
There's a lot of love.

I have a lot of love.
When I was a little girl, we used to get gifts from the Salvation Army. Things
like that are really very important. I've never seen so many smiles in my life.
I had never watched a porn—
I still haven't I remember the girls being really, really beautiful.
But there is nothing like the reaction of thousands of screaming fans.

Let me backtrack: the fans
used to say to me, "Why did you quit?" That's love.
It's a beautiful
thing.
I had a really, really bad vision of porn.
But it changed my life.

I don't know what's going to come tomorrow, that's how I've always lived my life.
I think it might be a shock, but I don't think I'll lose any fans:
a year ago I did a little movie, six scenes of straight porn.
I analogize it much like the Tina Turner story. I love
her. Let me say that, in retrospect, it is a truly incredible thing.
It's beautiful.

I feel like a beautiful
woman. I'm above the ring. Best times of my life.
I'm not saying I'm a slut or anything,
but I saw a lot of dick, ok? All of my fans
from wrestling have embraced me. I really feel like I'm loved.
Doing porn,

people say, "Why would you do porn?"
I've had much worse dates! They make it look so beautiful.
I did all these things that were very, very successful, and I loved
doing every single one of them. That was one of the highlights of my life.
It's a very welcoming business, it's just wonderful. The fans
are crazy. It's a wonderful thing.

I haven't been eating as much, doing the whole partying thing.
I really am happy, I'm doing really well right now. The fans
are always there no matter what you do. I hope that I affected somebody's life.

RAJON: RONDEAU

Rajon Rondo

Guys smile on the floor sometimes—well, I don't.
I spend most of my life alone.
Everybody else really doesn't know me.
I might be coming out with an R&B CD,
But what I do best is run the show.

That's how
It is, man. I got in the show-
Er and something was telling me:
Nobody remembers a loser.

I would make moves in the grocery store.
I've done some work before.
I envision people around me,
Whether it's a garbage can or an old lady walking down the street.
I miss being out there on the court.
Nobody remembers a loser.

ABUSE OF RACQUET

John McEnroe

Bullshit.
That ball's fucking
Out of bounds.

It was right on the line.
No mistakes so far in this match
Right?
You haven't
Overruled anything.
No mistakes whatsoever?
Answer my question.
The question, jerk.

Why don't we just
Call the match?
That's it?
It's only a game?

You can't be serious, man.
Excuse me?
You cannot be serious.
That ball was on the line.
Chalk flew up!
It was clearly in.
How can you possibly
Call that out?
Everyone knows it's in.
In this whole stadium.
And you call it out?
You guys are the absolute
Pits of the world.

I wasn't even talking to you,
Umpire.
I said it to my—

I wasn't talking to you,
Umpire.
Do you hear me?
I was talking to myself.
What did I say,
Umpire?
Tell me.
Please tell me.
Please tell me.

THE HISTORY OF WESTERN CIVILIZATION

Bill Walton

What a pathetic performance by this sad human being, this is a classic underachiever, this is a disgrace to the game of basketball and to the NBA, this guy has ruined every situation he has been in, he played like a disgrace tonight, he missed the two worst shot attempts in the history of Western Civilization, nobody is going to tell him he has to go back to Iran, his arrogance is an insult to people who think, show some respect, think of Beethoven in the age of the Romantics, the only way this hall of famer is getting into the hall of fame is if he pays the $5.99 admission fee, and the only thing he's worth is another team's mistake.

He added muscle and bulk from pushing that steel and treating this game like a buffet line, he couldn't get himself away from the buffet table, stumbling out there, dazed and confused, this winner of the genetic lottery, that incredible computer generated body he has may be a violation of all the basic rules of human decency, he has just completely changed the fate of Western Civilization here, who knows how many pounds on that big beautiful body of his, this guy is cut from stone, you realize what a classical human being he is, as if Michelangelo was reading and a lightning bolt flashed before him.

So this is what it's come to, a celebration of basketball, a celebration of life itself: the vision, the creativity, the gentleness of spirit, he has it all, one of the greats—not just of this generation, but of all time—doing things we've never seen from anybody, from any planet, it will say on his tombstone, "His left leg belongs in the Smithsonian," like walking through Yosemite with John Muir, coming down the Grand Canyon with John Wesley Powell, standing at Gettysburg with Abraham Lincoln, we celebrate his brilliance, he is just a beautiful person inside and out, a very likeable person once you get to know him, one of the true marvels, not just of basketball, or in America, but in the history of Western Civilization.

WE DON'T DO THINGS WE AREN'T GOOD AT BY NATURE

Danica Patrick

In the Lamborghini I have to avoid certain roads because of potholes,
and there's nowhere to put my drink, no cup holder.
I'm not going to lie, it looks pretentious.
I used to think it was cool to drive it to dinner.
Now? Like I really need to be looked at anymore.

MY NAME'S TONY HAWK, I'M A PROFESSIONAL SKATEBOARDER

Tony Hawk

A hardcore street skater doesn't care
About the spinning thing,
If someone's going
To do a 1080 or not—that's not even on his radar.
When I was growing up, we would just go out and skate together.
None of us have spun three times around on anything.
If you're going to go on the scale of spinning,
The public understands vertical skating easier.
Am I an extremist? I don't know.
I would leave that up to other people to decide.
Do I really have to apologize to gravity for that?
It's like I'm a businessman. My official title is C.E.O.
It's not like you fall a great height.
I had a pretty tough time this fall. Gravity got me back.

EL VILLANO

Dave "Tiger" Williams

They call me Tiger because I'm tough on the ice.
Nothing's ever over for me. You gotta be hot.
Then, when I'm home, I try to be nice.

When the coach asked, "Who's gonna be the tough guy?"
I was dumb enough to beat somebody off.
They call me Tiger because I'm tough on the ice.

I never said fight. Did I use the word fight?
Let's have some balls and stir up the pot.
Then, when I'm home, I try to be nice.

I don't know why everybody gets excited.
I'd rather see *Starsky & Hutch* get cut off.
They call me Tiger because I'm tough on the ice.

Whether you're the good guy or the bad guy,
It sounds like I'm Charlie Manson's broth-
er. They call me Tiger because I'm tough on the ice.
Then, when I'm home, I try to be nice.

I, BEST

George Best

I've been kicking since I was one year old.
I have lovely memories of home.
I was the same as all the other kids.
I was the only kid who kept his vest on.
I was just another player.
I was only learning.
I had a dream that came true.
I just looked forward to going out to play so much.
I always felt like an entertainer out there.
I think I can remember almost every goal I scored.
I scored from a corner.
I knew I'd scored a great goal.
I used to do things like that for fun.
I was only starting.
I enjoyed being one of the boys.
I liked being a man's man.
I also happened to enjoy women's company.
I think everybody knows I like Swedish girls.
I like screwing, all right?
I'd have a go at anything.
I think balance is very important.
I always got sent off for silly things.
I started to have a lot of doubts.
I fought it and fought it and fought it.
I didn't know what was going on.
I learnt too late.
I still have dreams about that split second when everything stood still.
I can't remember much about it.
I just kept running until I saw space.
I'd let them down as well as myself of course.
I went back on my own.
I came back and I basically didn't know what to do.
I came back and faced the same sort of problems.
I don't want to face any more problems.
I don't actually believe that nothing's impossible.

I don't expect it, but it's a fact of life.
I never played in a Cup Final or a World Cup.
I would have loved to.
I've still got a little bit of a way to go.

THE DEILIAD

Deion Sanders

1.

Deion,

Do you know what you've done?

You've excited those people.
You've done everything that you wanted to do.

One thing, Deion Sanders—
he has a great relationship

with the Lord.

2.

I'm happy. I mean,
This is where my life has matriculated to.
Just being a blessing to others.
God has blessed me to be a blessing.
And I have a high school.

I've opened nightclubs,
I've opened many various things.
It's a way of life.
That's when you know I'm successful.
Just life.

3.

I'm 100% football
and I plan to put everything into football.
Football is such an analogy of life.

Defeating the opposition—there's
always an opposition in life.

They have something
that you call unnecessary roughness;
you do that in life as well.
There's some things in life
that are so *unnecessary*.

4.

Now you got all the answers.
You got the keys to unlock
every engine and every car door and every obstacle
in life
that could warrant your attention.

You start to fathom in your mind,
to disseminate who's who…
That's a scary place.

Sometimes resources
in the hands of a fool
would be a fool.
I'm not just going to say the pressure.
The know-how. The wherewithal.

Trials and tribulations.

5.

I observe my butt off, man.

I was a kid
who learned a lot
watching television,
believe it or not.

I saw a young
African-American entrepreneur
named George Jefferson
that started a business,
a dry cleaning business.

But he moved
on up.

6.

Sporadically and quickly,
we decided we had to tell our story.

Everything is a microwave life right now.
We can all garnish and make money.
We're not dreaming anymore.
Everyone wants to go up the stairs
but they don't want to go take the process.

You're just hearing about it
outwardly and abroad
because of the severity of it.

We all make a tremendous
amount of decisions.
I feel like I made some great decisions.
And timely decisions.
And cautionary decisions.

We now see
the other way around:
a few others burning in the furnace
and so many other values
that people deem
to set a candor on.

7.

What is this besides bait?
Let me manipulate you with this bait.

I would only imagine
the people I could have touched.

I want you to understand who I am, what I am,
and how I am
and where I'm going
and how to get there.

Everything is everything.

I can't be an alleged guy
that's lost his mind.
That's not who I am.
That's not what I am.

You can't hide who you are anymore
without living a lie.

Try your best, man,
but you gotta be you.

POSTGAME

SOFT LIKE CHARMIN

Nick Young (aka Swaggy P)

1.

Just gotta do
What I gotta do
And when I gotta do it.
You know,
So basically
Just doing what I gotta do
Every time I step on the court,
Do what I gotta do.
So, I'm just doing what I do.

Just, you know, when
I touch the ball
I just do what I gotta do.
That's going in the hole.
You know, shots go up
And, you know,
I just do.

It's kinda like,
I can't even think about it
But I'm just doing what I gotta do,
Just like I been saying,
You know,
It's hard to guard somebody,
You know,
Like myself.
It's tough.
But I'm not here to talk about that.
Let's talk about me
doing what I gotta do.

2.

When I'm out there
I don't play like Charmin.
I play like Scott.
I like Scott tissue.
It's a little rougher,
You know.
No, I don't like Ultra Soft.
It breaks.
And it's too soft in your hands.

Guns and Roses.
Slash.
I kinda play like Slash,
You know.
It's Slash, right?
Slash?

I can't be Axl Rose,
The head dude.
I'm in the back,
Playing the guitar,
You know.
He's kind of known 'cause
He do wild stuff
So that's like me.

3.

I'm glad we won
I ain't gonna lie to you.
I'm glad I got the chance to hit a
Game winner.
With somebody like Kobe on the floor
Who usually has the ball in his hand all the time.
You know.
Let him have a day off.

Take a break.
I said,
"Take a break, little man,
You kind of tired."
You know
And, he was playing point guard,
He was huffing and puffing
And I'm like,
"I got this, brother.
I got this."

And I had a epiphany,
That it was like *The Sixth Man*.
You ever seen *The Sixth Man*?
I had bright lights shining,
Bright lights shining on me,
I just felt like the glow was on me.
It was crazy.

Once it left my hands
I kinda knew it was cash.
I'm like, I don't miss.
That's my new name.
IDM.
Call me, IDM.
I Don't Miss.

You feel me?

RUSSIA BETTER CANADA

Nail Yakupov

We win first.
We win Canada second.
We win—we win Canada third win.
And eighty thousand peoples.
Red jersey everybody put red and white jersey.
Why we win we score more goals.
And it doesn't matter how much
How many shoots Canada.
Shoot our pucks our nets we're win.
We're pretty excited and
It doesn't matter right now.
We win.
We beat Canada.

I don't know.
You can give me like 100 questions
But we win.
Russia win.
Russia better Canada.
So.
See you next time.

Surprise tonight?
Not surprise.
We prepare one hundred percent.
We score six goals.
We score more goals.
We win the games.
We win Canada.
We beat Canada.
We win.
Wonderful rink eighty thousand guys.
Canada! Canada, let's go!
We have—I think we have—
thirty, forty guys Russian guys from Siberia.

And they put their Russian jersey
And *Come on, Russiaaaaaaaa!*
And we win.
So that's it.
Thanks guys.

THREE YARDS AND A CLOUD OF DUST

Woody Hayes

We do want to win
Because winning
Is the epitome of team effort.
And we must keep that
And we must inculcate that
Into our football players.

He has to be team-oriented.
Usually, he comes from a good home.
He comes from a home
That has respected him as a youngster.
And he's learned to have self-esteem
Because he was esteemed in that home.

The older I get
And I shouldn't say this
Because it'll always be misconstrued
But the older I get the less
I care about what they say.
Sorry. I have to level with
Woody Hayes, but I don't
Have to level with them.
As long as I feel I'm treating
These youngsters right
And I'm trying honestly to
Help them get an education
Why, I don't care much
What they say.
Because I'll step into their classroom
And do a better job there
Than they'll ever do on the
Football field.

There are three things that can happen
When you pass,

And two of them ain't good.
I'm not trying to win a popularity poll.
I'm trying to win football games.
The minute I think I'm getting mellow,
I'm retiring.
Who ever heard of a mellow winner?

I wanted that undefeated season
More than anything
I ever wanted in my life.
I'd give anything—
my house, my bank account,
anything but my wife and family—
to get it.

You had better
Go ahead and fire me.
Nobody despises to lose
More than I do.
That's got me into trouble
Over the years,
But it also made a man
Of mediocre ability
Into a pretty good coach.

MAPLE WORLD PASTA

Metta World Peace

There's no various nothing.
He had elbow pasta,
And I had shell pasta
And I told him how my shell pasta
Was better than his elbow pasta,
And he was pretty upset about that.
He loves elbow pasta,
But I disagree.
I think shell pasta is better.
I don't care.
I will stand by that.
Shell pasta.

It's like when your son is doing bad in math class.
Your goal for him does not change, right?
You still want him to be a really good kid, right?
And good at math.
"Go do it, son!"
That's how we are here:
"Do it, Knicks! Do it!"

We're not struggling.
It's part of life.
You know how life is.
We had a bad hair day.

I honestly didn't even know
Who the coach was
When I was coming
To New York.
I just wanted
To win a championship.
I didn't even know
who was coaching.
I didn't care.

It could have been
Aunt Jemima.
They could have had
The syrup coaching.

VERY HARD WORDS

Zinedine Zidane

You hear them once and
You try to move away.
But then you hear them twice,
And then a third time.
I am a man and some words
Are harder to hear than actions.
I would rather have
Taken a blow to the face than hear that.
Do you imagine that
In a World Cup final,
With just ten minutes to go
To the end of my career,
I am going to do something
Like that because
It gives me pleasure?
It was inexcusable.
I apologize.
But I can't regret what I did
Because it would mean
That he was right
To say all that.

I DON'T EAT HAIR

Pete Rose

1.

I picked the wrong vice.
I should have picked alcohol.
I should have picked drugs or
I should have picked beating up my wife
or girlfriend
because if you do those three,
you get a second chance.

2.

I was feeling sorry for myself
when I compared my vice to others,
including abuse and drinking.
Of course, all vices
are not to be excused.

KERRIGAN V. HARDING

Tonya Harding (ft. Nancy Kerrigan)

I would like to begin by saying
how sorry I am
about what happened to Nancy Kerrigan.

I'm embarrassed and ashamed
to think that anyone close to me
could be involved.

I just ask forgiveness.
She has her life
and I have my life.

Everybody has bad days
and I guess both her
and I had bad days.

I know what I'm capable of
and I hope everyone here in this room
knows what I'm capable of.

If you want to get rid of me—
tough,
it isn't going to happen.

Somebody wants to know
something about me
they should ask me themselves.

Everybody out there to me
is basically the same.
If I have something on my mind

I'll say it.
I don't ever hold back
on anything.

Sometimes
that gets me into trouble,
but most of the time it doesn't.

I never get to talk about this stuff.

Why?

I'm not the picture-perfect
type of girl
or whatever.

I quit school my sophomore year.
I didn't have boyfriends;
I didn't really have any friends.

I worked as an assistant manager
at a restaurant and I skated.
That's all I had.

Those became pretty
dark days for me.
Still are.

Falling in love with skating
was the challenge,
I guess.

I had everything on the line
and I
did it.

I was basically perfect.
Everybody else made mistakes.
I didn't make any mistakes.

That was my year.

You just know the feeling.
I can't describe the feeling

of how it felt.
There was people standing up
giving me a standing ovation.

For the very first time,
I just knew:
I knew I was the best.

That was the best I've ever been.

Why?

My sister, when she was thirteen
she ran away from home
and became a streetwalker.

And now she's living in Hawaii
or something like that
with some Chinese guy.

I'm really different from my brother
because he used to steal a lot of things
and he still does.

He's like my mom.
My relationship with my mom is really bad.
She's a good mother

but she's not a good mother.
She hits me and she beats me
and she drinks.

She left me with my father.
She didn't want me. She told him,
"I don't want her, you take her."

I just had enough of my life,
of being beat up, put down,
telling me that I'm not going

to amount to anything in my life.
I was told that my whole entire life
by my mother.

I just had enough. It was horrible.
Finally they gave in
because I was crying.

I wanted to be
the first woman
to ever do something.

And now I have nothing.

Why?

I've tried to put the past behind me
And now today I feel like
I can start a fresh new life.

Everything that's happened to me
has made me into
who I am today.

If you don't like who I am today,
well,
tough.

Look at me:
I'm a female boxer.
Woo-hoo.

Whether people boo me

or cheer me
it doesn't matter.

I'm done with that. I'm taking care of me.
I'm not an educated woman.
This is my whole life.

There's been a couple of times
where maybe I shouldn't
have been here anymore.

You just gotta keep going.
That's what life is, I guess.
It's all a game. It's all fake.

It doesn't matter what I do,
I know I was the best—
at one point.

Until I die,
and even after I'm dead,
people are still going to make money

because my name is Tonya Harding.

HIGH SCHOOL BLITZ

Apollos Hester

At first we started slow,
We started real slow.
And that's all right
That's okay
Because sometimes in life
You're going to start slow.

We told ourselves,
We're going to start slow
But we're always always
Going to finish fast.
No matter what the score was
We're going to finish hard
We're going to finish fast.

They had us the first half,
I'm not gonna lie.
They had us.
We weren't defeated
But they had us.

It took guts
It took an attitude.
That's all it takes
That's all it takes
To be successful
Is an attitude.

It's an awesome feeling
It's an awesome feeling
When you truly believe
That you're going to be successful
Regardless of the situation
Regardless of the scoreboard
You are going to be successful

Because you put in
All the time
All the effort
All the hard work.

And you know that it's
going to pay off.
And if it doesn't pay off
You continue to give God the glory.
If you still lose the game,
You continue
To get each other's back.

And that's what we realized.
Win or lose,
We realized that
We were going to be
All right.
And it was gonna be okay.
We were gonna keep smiling.

It was awesome.
Awesome.
Awesome.

GOOD GAME

Rasheed Wallace

It was a good game.
Both teams played hard.

Both teams
Played hard,
My man.

Both
Teams
Played
Hard.

Both teams played hard.
God bless and good night.

"AUTHOR" BIOS

Pasha Malla is the author of four books and a past contributor to *Esquire*, *McSweeney's*, Newyorker.com, *Salon* and *Slate*, as well as the *Undisputed Guide to Pro Basketball History*. He lives in Canada.

Jeff Parker's books include *Where Bears Roam the Streets: A Russian Journal*, the novel *Ovenman*, and the short story collection *The Taste of Penny*. He teaches in the MFA Program for Poets & Writers at the University of Massachusetts Amherst.

featherproof BOOKS

*Publishing strange and beautiful fiction and nonfiction
and post-, trans-, and inter-genre tragicomedy.*

SLAM DUNKS

Available at bookstores everywhere, and direct from Chicago, Illinois at

www.*featherproof*.com